A Dorling Kindersley Book

Project Editors Scott Steedman and Laura Buller
Art Editors Christopher Howson and Peter Bailey
Production Louise Barratt
Photography Clive Streeter

First published in Great Britain in 1992 by Dorling
Kindersley Publishers Limited, 9 Henrietta Street,
London WC2E 8PS
Copyright © 1992 *illustrations*
Dorling Kindersley Limited, London
Copyright © 1992 *text* Neil Ardley

**British Library Cataloguing in Publication
Data is available**

ISBN 0-86318-686-6

Reproduced in Hong Kong by Bright Arts
Printed in Belgium by Proost

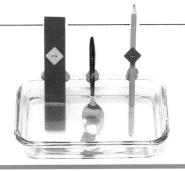

MY
SCIENCE
BOOK OF
HOT & COLD

Written by
Neil Ardley

DK

Dorling Kindersley
London • New York • Stuttgart

What are hot and cold?

Fires and summer days are hot, and ice cream and winter nights are cold. Hot and cold are caused by the same thing – heat. Cold objects just contain less heat than hot ones. Your body is warm because it contains a lot of heat. If you dive into a cold lake, you lose some of this heat.

Heat keeps us – and all living things – alive. Our bodies couldn't work without it. We need heat to cook food and to keep our homes warm. The Sun and the food we eat give us most of the heat we need to survive. We can also make heat by burning fuels like petrol and gas.

Cold snap
Water freezes if it gets very cold. When water loses a lot of heat it changes, and becomes ice. Snow is made up of tiny ice crystals.

Eat for heat
Cooking changes food. It can make the food tastier, and easier to eat. The food then changes again inside us. It produces heat that warms our bodies.

Heat from nowhere
Whenever two things rub together, heat is produced. Try rubbing your hands together if they're cold. It's an easy way to warm up!

Burning up
Fires need heat to start. The heat from one fire may make more fires break out. In the woods, the flames spread from tree to tree, and vast forests may burn down.

Be warm or be cool
Layers of clothes keep you warm in cold weather because they trap your body heat. Lightweight clothes help you to stay cool in hot weather. They let some heat escape.

⚠ This sign means **take care**. You should ask an adult to help you with this step of the experiment.

Be a safe scientist
Follow all the directions carefully and always take care, especially with glass, scissors, matches, candles, and electricity. Never put anything in your mouth or eyes.

Take care when handling hot objects such as hairdriers and hot taps. Make sure warm water is not too hot to touch, and ask an adult to help you use hot water.

Heat trap

Build a heat trap and capture some heat from the Sun. Rays of heat travel from the Sun to the Earth. The heat trap catches and holds this heat.

You will need:

Glass of water

Aluminium foil

Ruler

Plastic wrap

Large cardboard box

Tape   Pen

Scissors

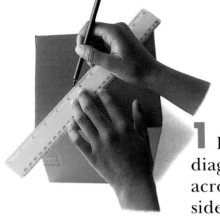

1 Draw matching diagonal lines across the short sides of the box.

2 Carefully cut the corners and most of one side off the box with the scissors.

Place the shiny side upwards.

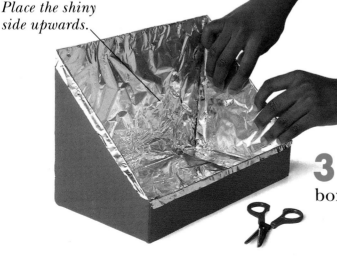

3 Line the inside of the box with aluminium foil.

Rays of heat from the Sun pass through the plastic wrap. They do not pass out again. The heat is trapped.

The heat "reflects" from, or bounces off, the foil.

4 Place the box somewhere sunny and put the glass of water inside it. Cover the box with plastic wrap.

The heat enters the water and makes it warm.

5 ⚠ The water soon gets warm. Test it with your finger and feel!

Growing under glass

Flowers grow well in a greenhouse. Heat passes through the glass walls and roof and is trapped inside, warming the air in the greenhouse, even on cold days.

Up and away

Heat can make things fly! This is because hot air rises. When air is heated and rises, the heat moves upward by "convection". Convection also helps heat to spread out from a heater to warm up a room.

You will need:

Very light plastic bag

Hairdrier

1 ⚠ Open the bag and hold it upside down. Ask a friend to point the hairdrier into the bag. Switch the hairdrier on.

The bag fills with hot air.

The hot air is light and rises, lifting the bag.

Keep your hands away from the stream of hot air.

2 After a few seconds, switch the hairdrier off and let go of the bag. It floats upwards.

Hot air power
Convection makes a hot-air balloon fly. A gas burner heats the air in the balloon. The hot air rises, lifting the balloon and the basket with it.

Sliding buttons

Put some objects in hot water and see which ones heat up. If heat flows through an object easily, the object is a good "conductor" of heat.

You will need:

Hot water

Plastic ruler

Wooden pencil

Butter

Glass dish

Metal spoon

Plasticine

Three buttons

1 Attach the ruler, spoon and pencil to the dish with plasticine.

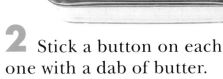

Line up the buttons.

2 Stick a button on each one with a dab of butter.

Heat does not travel through wood or plastic well.

3 ⚠ Gently fill the dish with hot water.

Heat travels through the metal spoon and melts the butter.

4 Soon one button slides into the water. The others do not move.

Bubbling bottle

Force air out of a bottle by heating it, then suck water back into the bottle by cooling it down. You will see how things get bigger when they are heated and smaller when they are cooled.

You will need:

Three bendy straws

Large dish

Glass of water

Jugs of warm and cold water

Sticky tape

Plasticine

Food colouring

Plastic bottle

1 Put a straw in the mouth of the bottle and press plasticine around it to make a tight seal.

2 Tape the other straws to the first one to form a long tube.

3 Colour the water in the glass with some food colouring.

4 Stand the bottle in the dish. Bend the tube so that the free end sticks into the glass of water.

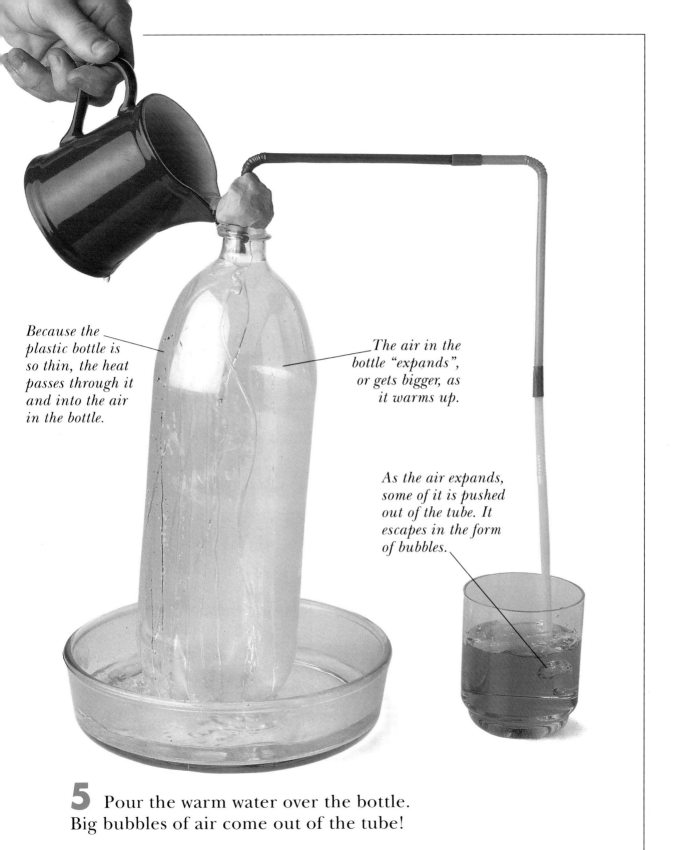

Because the plastic bottle is so thin, the heat passes through it and into the air in the bottle.

The air in the bottle "expands", or gets bigger, as it warms up.

As the air expands, some of it is pushed out of the tube. It escapes in the form of bubbles.

5 Pour the warm water over the bottle. Big bubbles of air come out of the tube!

Continued on next page

Air in the bottle *"contracts", or gets smaller, as it cools.*

6 Now pour the cold water over the bottle. The coloured water is drawn up the tube and into the bottle.

Water takes up the space left as the air in the bottle contracts.

Coming unstuck

Do you know the best way to loosen a lid that is stuck on a jar? Hold it under a stream of hot water. The heat makes the lid expand a little so that it does not grip the jar so tightly. The lid should then unscrew.

Continued from previous page

Hold up

Pick up a cup with a balloon! Warm and cold water will do the trick, by making air expand and then contract.

1 Pour some warm water into the plastic cup.

The warm water makes the air in the cup expand.

2 Blow up the balloon. Pour some cold water over it.

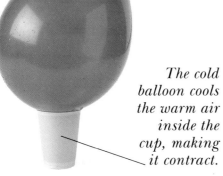

The cold balloon cools the warm air inside the cup, making it contract.

3 Empty the cup. Then press the balloon down on it firmly.

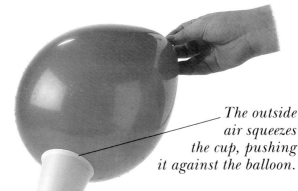

The outside air squeezes the cup, pushing it against the balloon.

4 After a minute, raise the balloon. It grips the cup, lifting it into the air!

Heat tester

Build a simple thermometer. It can test how hot or cold things are. A thermometer measures the "temperature", which goes up or down as things get hotter or colder.

You will need:

 Clear straw

 Plasticine

Colouring pens

Card

Scissors

 Cold water

 Food colouring

Glass bottle

1 Pour cold water into the bottle until it is three-quarters full. Then add a few drops of food colouring.

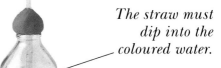

The straw must dip into the coloured water.

2 Put the straw into the bottle and seal it in place with some plasticine.

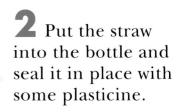

Use a black pen to mark the level.

3 Blow gently into the bottle until the water rises halfway up the straw.

4 Cut two sets of slits in the card. Slide it over the straw. Mark the level of the water. This is your thermometer.

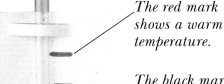
The red mark shows a warm temperature.

The black mark shows a normal temperature.

The blue mark shows a cool temperature.

Heat from the lamp makes the air in the bottle expand. The air pushes the water up the straw.

When the air in the bottle cools, it contracts and sucks the water back.

5 Put the thermometer in a warm place, such as under a lamp. Now the level rises. Mark it with a red pen.

6 Put the thermometer in the refrigerator for 10 minutes. The level falls. Mark it in blue.

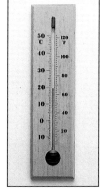

Twin scales
The tube on this thermometer contains red liquid, which moves up or down a scale to indicate the temperature. It uses two temperature scales – Celsius (C), and Fahrenheit (F).

Coming clean

You can clean some dirty water, just by heating it up and cooling it down! Heat changes a liquid like water into an invisible vapour. When you cool this vapour, it changes back into clear, liquid water.

You will need:

Plastic wrap

Small glass

Deep dish

Spoon

Scissors

Sticky tape

Ice cubes

Soil

Warm water

1 Put the soil in the deep dish. Add the warm water and stir with the spoon.

The rim must be above the dirty water.

2 Put the glass in the centre of the dish.

3 Cover the dish with plastic wrap and tape it in place.

4 Place the ice cubes in the centre of the plastic wrap.

When the water vapour hits the cool wrap, it changes back into liquid water.

5 Leave the dish for a short time. Water drops form on the inside of the wrap and drip into the glass.

Heat causes some water to change into vapour, which rises into the air.

Try increasing the heat by sitting the bowl in the Sun.

6 Take out the glass. The water in it is clean!

The dirt does not turn to vapour, so the water in the glass is not dirty.

Out of oil

Crude oil is made up of petrol and many other liquids. In an oil refinery, the liquids are separated by heating the oil. All the liquids change into vapours. Each kind of vapour is then cooled separately to form a pure liquid, such as petrol.

Brief candle

Heat can make things catch fire, but only when there is oxygen. You can light a candle and then put it out as if by magic. Just take away its oxygen supply.

You will need:

Tablespoon

Matches

Candle

Vinegar

Glass dish

Baking powder

Plasticine

1 Stick the candle to the bottom of the dish with plasticine.

Make sure the candle is not taller than the dish.

2 Sprinkle a tablespoon of baking powder around the candle.

When heated by the flame, the wax in the wick takes in oxygen from the air and the candle burns.

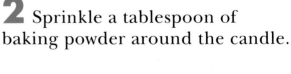

3 ⚠ Ask an adult to light the candle with a match.

4 Add a tablespoon of vinegar. The baking powder begins to froth.

The froth should not reach the flame.

The vinegar plus the sodium bicarbonate in the baking powder produce bubbles of carbon dioxide gas.

5 Wait. Suddenly, the flame goes out!

The invisible carbon dioxide covers the flame and smothers it.

6 ⚠ Try lighting the candle again. The match goes out before it reaches the candle!

Fighting fire
Covering a fire with carbon dioxide or foam puts it out. The layer of gas or foam stops air from reaching the flames. Without oxygen from the air, the fire goes out.

Heat store

Hot things soon lose their heat and get cool if they are not "insulated". An insulator does not let heat pass through it easily. Keep some water warm by making an insulated container.

You will need:

Big jar with lid

Small jar with lid

Small glass

Warm water

Sticky tape

Wide cork

Scissors

Aluminium foil

Put the shiny sides inwards.

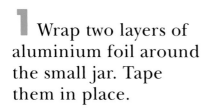

1 Wrap two layers of aluminium foil around the small jar. Tape them in place.

2 ⚠ Pour warm water into the glass and the small jar. Twist the lid on to the jar.

3 Put the cork on the bottom of the big jar and sit the small jar on top of it. Then twist the lid on to the big jar. This is your heat store.

The lids of the jars help to stop heat escaping upwards.

The shiny layers of foil help to keep in the heat.

Heat cannot travel well through the cork or the layer of air around the bottle.

Heat easily leaves the glass, so the water cools.

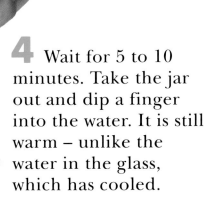

4 Wait for 5 to 10 minutes. Take the jar out and dip a finger into the water. It is still warm – unlike the water in the glass, which has cooled.

Keeping hot – and cold

Drinks stay hot in a vacuum flask. It has a shiny lining and tight seals. These don't allow much heat to escape. The flask also keeps cool drinks cool, because heat cannot get into it.

Flower pot fridge

Can you make a refrigerator from a flower pot, to keep a drink cool on a hot day? The wet flowerpot becomes cold as the hot Sun makes the water turn into vapour, or "evaporate".

1 Put the can of drink in the dish.

As the water evaporates, it takes heat away from the pot, so the drink gets cooler.

2 Cover the can with the flower pot. Pour water over the sides of the pot.

Make sure there is plenty of water in the dish.

3 Place the dish and pot in a sunny place. The wet pot gets colder and cools the drink.

4 After about an hour, lift up the pot. The drink will be cold enough to cool you down!

Setting solid

A liquid changes to a solid, or freezes, when it gets very cold. Water turns to ice when its temperature falls to its "freezing point". See how salt changes the freezing point of water.

Ice tray

Salt

Paper napkin

Two coloured paper clips

Jug of water

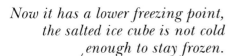

1 Bend the paper clips. Put them in the ice tray, and cover them with water. Freeze to make ice cubes.

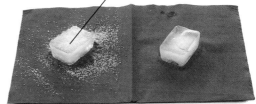

Adding salt to the ice lowers its freezing point.

2 Put two paper napkins on a table. Place an ice cube on each one. Sprinkle salt on one ice cube.

Now it has a lower freezing point, the salted ice cube is not cold enough to stay frozen.

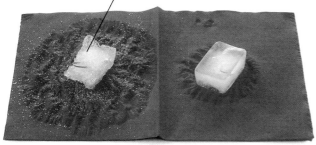

3 The salted cube melts fastest. The paper around it gets very wet and the paper clip begins to show. The other cube melts more slowly.

Wintry seas
Waves still break on this snow-covered shore. The sea does not freeze here, even though it is very cold. This is because sea water is salty.

Slicing the ice

Can you cut right through an ice cube without dividing it in two? Try this amazing trick and find an unusual way to melt ice.

You will need:

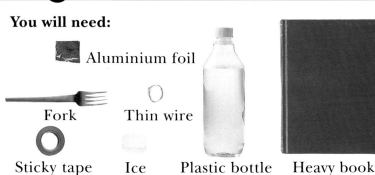

Aluminium foil

Fork

Thin wire

Sticky tape

Ice cube

Plastic bottle full of water

Heavy book

The fork must not be able to move.

1 Tape the handle of the fork to the edge of a table. Place the book on top of the handle.

Make sure the wire doesn't slip off the bottle neck.

2 ⚠ Carefully twist the ends of the wire around the bottle neck to form a loop.

3 Put a square of foil on the prongs of the fork. Sit the ice cube on top.

The wire pulls down very hard. This makes the ice melt just beneath the wire.

4 Loop the wire over the ice cube. The weight of the bottle is now pulling the wire into the ice cube.

After the wire passes, the pressure is removed and the water freezes again.

5 Watch as the wire slices through the ice.

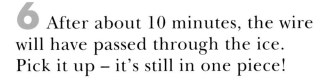

6 After about 10 minutes, the wire will have passed through the ice. Pick it up – it's still in one piece!

Fast on the feet
When skaters skim over the ice, their weight presses down on the blades. A slippery film of water forms where the blades press on the ice. The film of water freezes again after the skaters pass.

Easy freeze

How can you freeze things without a freezer? Find out how ice and salt can make things very cold – and end up with some tasty ice cream!

You will need:

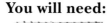
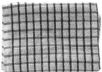
Tea towel

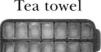
Ice cubes

Drinking chocolate powder

Salt

Large bowl

Glass

Milk

Cream

Tablespoon

1 In the glass, mix one tablespoon of drinking chocolate, two tablespoons of milk and one tablespoon of cream.

Use the spoon to mix the ingredients well.

2 Put a layer of ice cubes into the bowl. Sprinkle with a lot of salt.

3 Place the glass on the layer of salted ice cubes.

4 Build up more layers of ice and salt around the glass.

5 Place the tea towel over the bowl. Leave the mixture in the bowl for about an hour, stirring it every few minutes.

The salt makes the ice melt quickly. The change from ice to water needs heat.

As heat is drawn from the mixture in the glass, the mixture gets very cold and freezes.

6 Have a taste of your home-made chocolate ice cream!

Growing ice

An icicle forms as water drips over the edge of a cold surface. Heat leaves the water, which turns to ice. The icicle grows as more water runs down the cold icicle and freezes.

Picture credits
(Picture credits abbreviation key: B=below, C=centre, L=left, R=right, T=top)

Heather Angel: 9BR; Lupe Cuhna Photo Library: 6CR; Robert Harding Picture Library: 10BL; The Image Bank/Andre Gallant: 27BL; Tony Stone Worldwide/David Austen: 7TR; Zefa Picture Library: 6TR, 25BL;/ Harlicek: 21BL;/H. Lütticke: 29C;/ Streichan: 19BR.

Picture research Kathy Lockley and Clive Webster

Science consultant Jack Challoner

Dorling Kindersley would like to thank Jenny Vaughan for editorial assistance; Mr Halpin, the staff and children of Harris City Technology College, London, especially Joel Edwards, James Jenkins, Chelene Jess, Faye Kester, Joanne McShane, Ian Millard, Jack Newton, Donna Shaw, Elahay Syed, Wayne Trunchion, Emma White; Ashley Giles, Paul May, and Sonia Opong.